CONTENTS

COUNTRY OVERVIEW:
BULGARIA AT A GLANCE

History

Bulgaria has a long and fascinating history that reaches back into antiquity. Bulgarians are proud of their history, and you will make rapid progress toward earning their respect if you are knowledgeable about it.

Slavic tribes settled in the Balkan Peninsula in the sixth and seventh centuries, followed a century later by the Proto-Bulgars, who conquered the Slavic tribes and founded the first Bulgarian kingdom in 681. The kingdom reached the height of its power in the ninth century and included most of the Balkan Peninsula. The royal capital at Turnovo was seized by the Turks in 1393, beginning nearly 500 years of Ottoman domination. During this period, Bulgaria's indigenous customs and values were preserved in monasteries and isolated mountain villages. In the 19th century, a strong national revival occurred, and the Russo-Turkish War of 1877–78 resulted in the restoration of self-government to Bulgaria.

Ferdinand of Saxe-Coburg-Gotha became Bulgaria's first monarch in 1887. He was forced to abdicate after World War I, and the throne passed to his son, Boris III. With the support of the army, Boris III imposed a dictatorship on the country in 1934. His death in 1943 left the country without a strong leader. In September 1944, the Soviet Union declared war on Bulgaria and quickly occupied its territory. In the aftermath of that war, Bulgarian communists seized power and abolished the monarchy, establishing the People's Republic of Bulgaria in 1946.

The communists initiated a planned economy based on the Soviet model, which collectivized agriculture and permitted rapid industrialization. After more than 44 years under this system, popular unrest and political turmoil culminated in the collapse of communism in 1990. Since then, Bulgaria's transition to a democratic government and market economy has not been without difficulties. Following weeks of popular protest and strikes after hyperinflation and the collapse of the banking system in 1996 and 1997, the ruling Socialist Party stepped down, and unprecedented general elections were held. The new government initiated difficult but necessary reforms that helped bring a level of economic and political stability.

In 2004, Bulgaria became a member state of the NATO alliance. From 2001 until 2005, the Simeon II National Movement was the leading political party. The son of King Boris III, who grew up in Spain and was a successful businessman, led it. The movement formed a government that continued the commitment to political and economic integration with the European Union, but was seen as not being able to deliver on all of the promises it made. The subsequent elections on June 25, 2005, sent seven different parties to Parliament, none winning enough majority seats to form a government. During the past several years, there has been a rising right-wing nationalist anti-minority movement in Bulgaria, with a small, but vocal and growing support base. In October 2006, Georgi Parvanov of the relatively moderate Socialist Party was re-elected president for a second term. This broad coalition government worked toward the January 2007 EU accession. The government has committed to continuing to work on the "development roadmap" that the EU and Bulgaria have agreed upon.

Government

The Constitution of Bulgaria, adopted on July 12, 1991, established the Republic of Bulgaria as a parliamentary democracy with universal suffrage at 18 years of age. The executive branch is composed primarily of the president, vice president, prime minister, and Council of Ministers. The president and vice president are elected by popular vote for five-year terms.

The prime minister chairs the Council of Ministers and is nominated by the president for confirmation by the National Assembly. The prime minister is normally proposed by the majority party or coalition in the National Assembly. Deputy prime ministers are nominated by the prime minister. The legislative branch is composed of a unicameral National Assembly, or *Narodno Sobranie*, of 240 seats. Members are elected by popular vote to serve four-year terms. The judicial branch is composed of the Supreme Administrative Court and the Supreme Court of Cassation, whose chairmen are appointed for seven-year terms by the president; and a constitutional court made up of 12 justices appointed or elected for nine-year terms. The legal system of civil and criminal law is based on Roman law.

Economy

Under the communist system, Bulgaria had a centrally planned economy in which the government set economic goals and directed production. Although this system worked effectively during the early stages of industrialization, it was inadequate for a more complex economy. With the fall of communism in 1990, Bulgaria began moving toward a free-market economic system.

The post-communist Bulgarian economy has encountered significant challenges. Former Soviet and Warsaw Pact markets, important for both imports and exports, disappeared. Embargoes on Iraq and Yugoslavia further reduced sources of fuel and foreign currency. Inflation and unemployment rose sharply, and food and fuel shortages became widespread. In an effort at revitalization, the government declared its support for a transition to a market-oriented system and began a far-reaching program of denationalization and privatization. Until recently, complex internal politics delayed privatization and structural reform.

The reform agenda was similar to that of other EU nations, but successive Bulgarian governments were not able to implement it. Between 1993 and 1996, privatization virtually stopped and elements of central planning (i.e., price controls, transfer of enterprises to state control, and political control over the central bank's policies) were restored. By late 1996, Bulgaria entered a period of catastrophic currency depreciation, runaway inflation, and economic collapse. In 1996, the Bulgarian economy endured its severest crisis since 1990: GDP declined by 10 percent, followed by a further 9.8 percent drop in the first half of 1997.

The year 1997 was one of profound economic and political changes. The establishment of the new democratic government in February brought stability and confidence to the country. Positive economic developments, such as growth in economic activities, increased foreign investment, stabilization of the financial sector, and strengthened inflation control, were reinforced with the introduction of the Currency Board in July 1997. By September, inflation was 3.6 percent, compared with 561.8 percent during the first three quarters of the year. Foreign reserves also grew substantially. The government adopted a long-term economic development program to achieve sustainable private sector and competition-led growth.

Hopes for continued economic progress, however, were derailed by events in Kosovo in 1998. Real GDP growth dropped to 0.5 percent in 1999. While exports were seriously curtailed, foreign direct investment managed to hold level with the amount of the previous year. In July 1999, the lev, the currency of Bulgaria, was revalued at 1:1 with the German mark. In December 1999, Bulgaria was invited to participate in EU accession talks. The country began chapter negotiations in January 2000. These negotiations on the 31 chapters were closed on June 15, 2004, and Bulgaria signed the Accession Treaty on April 25, 2005. Bulgaria joined the EU on January 2, 2007, and continues to work toward reforms aimed at eliminating corruption, reducing crime, tightening border control, improving government administration, strengthening the rule of law, and increasing the efficiency of the judicial systems. Even with EU accession, many Bulgarians still struggle to make ends meet as they cope with the impact of economic reform. While most Bulgarians are proud that they have become EU members, many are struggling with inflation, stagnant or slowly increasing salaries that cannot keep up with prices, and possible increased regulation.

People and Culture

Ethnic Bulgarians are descendants of the Slavs who settled in the region in the sixth century. The country's name comes from the Bulgars, a nomadic people from Central Asia who arrived a century later. They conquered the Slavs and together created the first Bulgarian kingdom. The largest minority groups within Bulgaria are Turkish (The government's efforts to forcibly assimilate ethnic Turks in the late 1980s caused many to flee the country), Bulgarian Muslims (ethnic Bulgarians who have converted to Islam are recognized as a separate group), and Romani (gypsy). Other minorities include Armenians, Greeks, Russians, and Jews.

Bulgaria's cultural life was rich during the Middle Ages. The Orthodox Church struggled to keep Bulgarian culture and tradition alive during the years of Ottoman rule. In the 19th century, Bulgaria's cultural life was influenced by both foreign models and native traditions. Bulgaria has developed particularly strong traditions in literature, music, and the arts, and has produced some world-famous opera singers.

Environment

The Danube River plateau produces wheat, corn, sugar beets, and sunflowers; while the Maritsa Valley produces tobacco and attar of roses, a key ingredient in perfume. Bulgaria's mountainous areas contain valuable forests, about three-quarters of which are broadleaf, with the remainder being coniferous. Bears, wolves, foxes, squirrels, elk, and wildcats still exist in these forests. In addition, several rare and endangered species of birds can be found in Bulgaria, particularly during the fall migrations.

Like much of Eastern Europe, Bulgaria has suffered for many years from heavy industrialization and poor pollution control. There have been some positive changes since the transition to a democratic government and market economy, though much of the reduction in pollution is due to the shutdown of factories. The poor condition of many cars, the lack of emission controls, and the use of soft coal for heating contribute to the current level of air pollution.

RESOURCES FOR FURTHER INFORMATION

Following is a list of websites for additional information about the Peace Corps and Bulgaria and to connect you to returned Volunteers and other invitees. Please keep in mind that although we try to make sure all these links are active and current, we cannot guarantee it. If you do not have access to the Internet, visit your local library. Libraries offer free Internet usage and often let you print information to take home.

A note of caution: As you surf the Internet, be aware that you may find bulletin boards and chat rooms in which people are free to express opinions about the Peace Corps based on their own experience, including comments by those who were unhappy with their choice to serve in the Peace Corps. These opinions are not those of the Peace Corps or the U.S. government, and we hope you will keep in mind that no two people experience their service in the same way.

General Information About Bulgaria

http://www.countrywatch.com/
On this site, you can learn anything from what time it is in Sofia to how to convert from the dollar to the **Bulgarian leva**. Just click on **Bulgaria** and go from there.

http://www.lonelyplanet.com/destinations
Visit this site for general travel advice about almost any country in the world.

http://www.state.gov/
The State Department's website issues background notes periodically about countries around the world. Find Bulgaria and learn more about its social and political history.

www.psr.keele.ac.uk/official.htm
This site includes links to all the official sites for governments worldwide.

www.geography.about.com/library/maps/blindex.htm
This online world atlas includes maps and geographical information, and each country page contains links to other sites, such as the Library of Congress, that contain comprehensive historical, social, and political background.

www.cyberschoolbus.un.org/infonation/info.asp
This United Nations site allows you to search for statistical information for member states of the U.N

www.worldinformation.com
This site provides an additional source of current and historical information about countries around the world.

Connect With Returned Volunteers and Other Invitees

www.rpcv.org
This is the site of the National Peace Corps Association, made up of returned Volunteers. On this site you can find links to all the Web pages of the "friends of" groups for most countries of service, made up of former Volunteers who served in those countries. There are also regional groups who frequently get together for social events and local volunteer activities.

www.peacecorpswriters.org
This site is hosted by a group of returned Volunteer writers. It is a monthly online publication of essays and Volunteer accounts of their Peace Corps service.

Online Articles/Current News Sites About Bulgaria

www.bulgaria-embassy.org
The site of the Bulgarian Embassy in Washington, D.C.

www.travel-bulgaria.com/explore/history.html
A travel site with information on Bulgarian history and culture.

www.sofiaecho.com/
The online version of Bulgaria's English language newspaper.

www.novinite.com
Sofia News Agency site with news in English.

http://www.vagabond-bg.com/

The website for an English language monthly magazine from Bulgaria.

International Development Sites About Bulgaria

http://www.undp.bg/
The United Nations Development Programme in Bulgaria.

www.usaid.gov/countries/bg/
Information about the U.S. Agency for International Development's work in Bulgaria. Note that the USAID mission in Bulgaria "graduated" Bulgaria, and the office closed in September 2008.

www.hrw.org/wr2k1/eurcpe/bulgaria.html
Human Rights Watch report on Bulgaria.

Recommended Books

1. Crampton, R.J. *A Short History of Modern Bulgaria.* Cambridge, England: Cambridge University Press, 1987.

2. Fonseca, Isabel. *Bury Me Standing: The Gypsies and Their Journey.* New York: Knopf, 1995.

3. Kaplan, Robert D. *Balkan Ghosts: A Journey Through History.* New York: St. Martin's Press, 1993.

4. Karklins, Rasma. *The System Made Me Do It: Corruption in Post-Communist Societies,* Armonk, N.Y.: M.E. Sharpe, Inc., 2005.

5. Kostich, Dragos D. *The Land and People of the Balkans: Albania, Bulgaria, Yugoslavia.* Philadelphia: J.B. Lippincott, 1962, 1973.

6. MacDermott, Mercia. *The Apostle of Freedom: A Portrait of Vasil Levsky.* London: Allen & Unwin, 1967.

7. Sanders, Irwin T. *Balkan Village.* Lexington: University of Kentucky Press, 1949.

8. Townson, Annabelle. *We Wait for You: Unheard Voices from Post-Communist Romania.* Lanham, Maryland: Hamilton Books, 2005 (paperback).

Books About the History of the Peace Corps
1. Hoffman, Elizabeth Cobbs. *All You Need is Love: The Peace Corps and the Spirit of the 1960's*. Cambridge, Mass.: Harvard University Press, 2000.

2. Rice, Gerald T. *The Bold Experiment: JFK's Peace Corps*. Notre Dame, Ind.: University of Notre Dame Press, 1985.

3. Stossel, Scott. *Sarge: The Life and Times of Sargent Shriver*. Washington, D.C.: Smithsonian Institution Press, 2004.

Books on the Volunteer Experience

1. Dirlam, Sharon. *Beyond Siberia: Two Years in a Forgotten Place*. Santa Barbara, Calif.: McSeas Books, 2004.

2. Casebolt, Marjorie DeMoss. *Margarita: A Guatemalan Peace Corps Experience*. Gig Harbor, Wash.: Red Apple Publishing, 2000.

3. Erdman, Sarah. *Nine Hills to Nambonkaha: Two Years in the Heart of an African Village*. New York, N.Y.: Picador, 2003.

4. Hessler, Peter. *River Town: Two Years on the Yangtze*. New York, N.Y.: Perennial, 2001.

5. Kennedy, Geraldine ed. *From the Center of the Earth: Stories out of the Peace Corps*. Santa Monica, Calif.: Clover Park Press, 1991.

6. Thompsen, Moritz. *Living Poor: A Peace Corps Chronicle*. Seattle, Wash.: University of Washington Press, 1997 (reprint).

LIVING CONDITIONS AND VOLUNTEER LIFESTYLE

Communications

Mail

Few countries in the world offer the level of mail service considered normal in the United States. If you expect U.S. standards for mail service, you will be in for some frustration. Mail sent via airmail typically takes three to four weeks, and packages sent by surface mail take from two to six months. Some mail may simply not arrive (fortunately, this is not a frequent occurrence, but it does happen). It is a good idea to advise family members that snail-mail can be sporadic.

Packages and letters arriving in Bulgaria are often checked by officials for dangerous items. The inspectors usually reseal the packages and letters and send them on, but there are reports of some never arriving at their destination and others arriving without money or expensive items that had been enclosed. Advise your family and friends to number their letters and include "Airmail" on their envelopes. (For letters, we recommend global airmail, available at U.S. post offices.)

We don't recommend that your friends and family declare large values for packages sent or insure them, as you may need to pay a tax to release packages of considerable value from customs.

After pre-service training, you will become a Volunteer and move to your site. Mail should then be addressed directly to you at your new residence. You can provide this information to family and friends toward the end of training, prior to moving to your site. If your residence does not provide for a secure or private mailbox, it may be better to have your personal mail sent to you at your work address.

It may be impractical to receive anything besides letters in the mail during training. Tell family and friends they should not send packages until after you have completed training and are at your assigned site. At that time, you will be better able to assess what things from home you really need and how best to have them sent. If you receive packages during training, you may also find it challenging to find space to store them at your host family's house and to transport these additional items to your permanent site.

Telephones

Your apartment may or may not have a landline telephone—many don't. For in-country calling, most Volunteers use mobile phones. During your first weeks of training, you will be given money for purchasing a mobile phone, which you will be expected to keep charged and with you throughout your service. Most Volunteers, however, find that talking for long periods of time on the phone is too expensive. Thus, Volunteers (and most Bulgarians) generally rely heavily on text messaging from cellphones, which is much cheaper than voice calls. All of the major Bulgarian cellular service providers also offer free text messaging from their Internet sites.

Standard long-distance telephone service is available but expensive. If you are calling on a landline from outside the capital, it may take a while to get a connection. Some calling cards from the United States (e.g., those issued by AT&T, MCI, and Sprint) can be used to call the United States. However, you cannot use these cards to call from Bulgaria to other countries because of a phone block in Bulgaria. There are multiple alternate providers that offer calls for just a few cents per minute from the U.S. to Bulgaria and from Sofia and a few other major cities in Bulgaria to the U.S., including "Foneca" and others. You can search for such services online, and usually purchase minutes using a credit card.

Most Volunteers who have home Internet access use Skype or VOIPStunt to call to the U.S. using their laptops. Those who don't, tend to call from an Internet club in their village or a nearby town or have family and friends in the U.S. call them. You alternatively can make international calls from a local public telephone or post office. The country code for Bulgaria is 359.

Computer, Internet, and Email Access
Some, but not all, Volunteers have access to computers at their worksites, which may or may not have Internet and email capabilities. Worksite equipment should, however, be used primarily for work-related activities, and you should not assume that it can be used for personal purposes. Internet and email access has become widely available throughout Bulgaria, and Internet cafes can be found in most towns, although they are generally not found in all rural villages. While it is likely you will have Internet access near your site, you should not assume that you will have constant email access. Advise family that in the case of a family emergency, they should contact the Peace Corps' Office of Special Services in Washington, D.C., which will then work to make quick contact with you.

The Peace Corps does not provide email accounts or technical and repair support. Repair services do exist in major towns and cities throughout Bulgaria, and service centers that represent some major computer manufacturers can be found in Sofia. Peace Corps does not replace computers in the case of loss or theft. If you do bring computer equipment, insurance is highly recommended.

Housing and Site Location

The Peace Corps staff uses an involved and thorough process to identify Volunteers' host organizations and towns. Potential host organizations fill out an in-depth application in which they state their reasons for wanting to work with a Volunteer, their organizational goals, how they see a Volunteer fitting into their organization, what specific work the Volunteer will assist with, desired skills, and available resources. Staff visits each site and discusses these items with the potential hosts, and ultimately uses a methodical system of evaluating potential sites based on community needs, the ability of Peace Corps Volunteers to help address those needs, the ability of a community to support a Volunteer, and the potential for a Volunteer to be successful at that site.

Toward the middle of your pre-service training (PST), the Peace Corps office and training staff match trainees and sites, and trainees learn where they will live and work for the next two years. Education, professional experience, and level of Bulgarian language ability are considered in matching individual Volunteers' skills with the needs of each site. While Volunteer interests are taken into account when possible, priority is given to local needs and how PCV skills match those needs. Volunteers should be prepared to serve in any region of Bulgaria on any assignment within their project area (YD, COD, or TEFL).

Housing is generally provided by a Volunteer's sponsoring organization. Most Volunteers live in a modest studio or one-bedroom apartment with plumbing, heating, and electricity. The range of available housing may vary greatly between Volunteers and sites. If you live in a town or city, you will likely live in an apartment in a communist-style housing "block," that, from the exterior, resembles the high-rises in public housing projects in U.S. cities.

Volunteers assigned to smaller communities should be prepared for the possibility of living in a private room in the home of a Bulgarian family. This can offer huge advantages, as you may be accepted into a local family and be "taken care of." Note that Bulgarian standards of privacy differ from those in the U.S. It is also common that landlords may leave some of their personal items in an apartment they are renting out.

Your heat source could be either one or more portable heaters, central heat, or wood-burning stoves in some rural areas. Heat and electricity are very expensive, and Bulgarians usually only heat the room they are currently in. They usually only turn on their hot water boiler when they are planning to take a shower. Expect it to be cold inside during the winter, and very hot during the summer. Indoor climate control concepts differ from what you are likely used to in the U.S.

Living Allowance and Money Management

You will receive a monthly living allowance that will enable you to maintain a modest lifestyle similar to that of average Bulgarians within your community. This allowance will be deposited in your bank account every month by Peace Corps/Bulgaria. It is intended to cover food, household supplies, local transportation, recreation, entertainment, and incidental expenses such as postage, film, reading material, stationery, and toiletries. In most cases, rent and utilities are paid by the sponsoring organization, but the Peace Corps assists with these expenses in some circumstances.

Most Volunteers in Bulgaria find their living allowance to be sufficient, as long as they live a frugal lifestyle. The lifestyle you adopt while serving in Bulgaria will determine how far your living allowance goes. These days in Bulgaria, there are many things to spend money on, and if you choose to eat frequently in restaurants, travel frequently, and buy imported food and toiletries, your living allowance likely will not last through each month. You may also have a harder time becoming a part of your community if you live at a higher economic level than the average community member. If you adopt a more typical average Bulgarian lifestyle, cook frequently, and choose primarily from the ample selections of local goods, your living allowance should be more than adequate.

Food and Diet

It is possible to eat a very healthy and natural diet in Bulgaria, if you prepare many of your own meals and use local foods. Larger towns and cities offer many of the same basic staples that you can find in the United States, with the exception of most prepared and instant foods. Volunteers in smaller towns sometimes experience shortages of certain items, especially in the winter, but there is typically an ample food supply if you are flexible about cooking with what is currently available. If you live in a small village, you may choose to occasionally shop in larger towns in your region, to fill in your food supplies and get items that are unavailable at your site.

Grilled meat and potatoes or salads best capture the essence of Bulgarian cuisine. Meals served in a family setting are heavy, oily, filling, and take hours to prepare. Many dishes are salty by American standards and Bulgarians cook with a lot of sunflower oil. Pork and chicken are the most popular meats—served roasted, breaded and fried, or grilled. The selection of seafood is limited, and it is advisable to refrain from eating it unless you know its origin. Seafood from the Danube or the Black Sea should generally not be eaten, while trout from mountain streams and fish raised on farms is generally safe to eat.

Vegetarians may get weary of eating breaded cheese, fried potatoes, or salad every time they go out for a meal or visit Bulgarian friends, but the abundance of wonderful fresh fruit and vegetables in season make it possible to prepare delicious meals at home. Prices of produce fluctuate greatly according to the season. Peppers, tomatoes, cucumbers, potatoes, cabbages, eggplants, zucchinis, and carrots are almost always available. However, in the winter in some communities, you may have to rely mainly on potatoes, cabbages, carrots, dried beans, and canned items. Locally grown fruits are available from late spring to late fall. During the winter, you may have to make do with canned fruits and fruit juice and imported fruits such as bananas, apples, and oranges.

Cereal and grains are available, although breakfast cereals can be expensive, as Bulgarians typically do not eat cereal for breakfast. The typical Bulgarian breakfast is banitza, a delicious pastry made from filo dough and cheese—which is made fresh daily in most towns and villages and costs around 50 U.S. cents. Bulgarians eat bread with every meal, and even most small towns have a place where you can buy freshly baked bread on a daily basis. Rice, pasta, and all-purpose white flour can also be purchased easily, but you will have to search extensively for whole-wheat flour. Various types of beans are widely available, and lentils are widely used. Dried soybean product was used in the past as a cheaper substitute for meat, and is available in specialty stores in the larger towns and cities. Milk is readily available. The two types of local cheese (white and yellow) are delicious and always available. Imported cheese is also available but expensive. Bulgarian yogurt, made primarily from cow and sheep milk, is a staple of Bulgarians, and is well known worldwide.

A cookbook of recipes to help you make the most of products available in Bulgaria will be given to you during training. You will be making a lot of things from scratch here, and if you do not already know how to cook, you will learn. Don't worry, before long you will be sharing your favorite recipes with others.

Transportation

Bulgaria has a large network of bus and train routes, which makes it possible to travel to practically all destinations by public transportation. Many Volunteers have experienced thefts while traveling, however, so you must be vigilant in protecting your valuables while using public transportation. Traveling on trams in Sofia requires extra vigilance. When traveling on trains, it is safest to travel in a compartment with a *baba* (grandmother).

Geography and Climate

Bulgaria is located in the Balkan Peninsula in southeastern Europe. The country is bordered by the Black Sea in the east, Turkey and Greece in the south, Macedonia and Serbia in the west, and Romania in the north. Although slightly larger than Tennessee, Bulgaria stands out as a land of great geographic and environmental diversity. The average elevation is 480 meters (1,584 feet) above sea level.

The country has four major geographic regions. The most northerly is the Danube plateau, which rises from the shores of the Danube River to the foothills in the east. Its climate is continental, with hot summers and cold winters. The second region is the Balkan Mountains (or *Stara Planina*, which means "Old Mountains" in Bulgarian), which extends across the center of the country and blocks cold winds from the plains of Russia. The third region, the valley drained by the Maritsa River in the south, has a Mediterranean climate with mild, rainy winters and warm, dry summers. South of the Maritsa Valley is the fourth region, the Rhodope Mountains, which forms the border between Bulgaria and Greece.

Bulgaria has a Mediterranean climate with four distinct seasons. As in the United States, weather patterns have been changing in recent years, so it is difficult to describe a "typical" year. Spring generally brings frequent rain. Spring and fall are temperate and feature beautiful flora. Summer temperatures average about 75 degrees Fahrenheit (24 degrees Celsius); but in July and August, they can reach the 90 F to 100 F range for a two-week period or longer. The highlands in the northeast are cooler than the more Mediterranean climate of the southwest. Bulgaria can get cold and gray in the winter, with temperatures averaging around 32 F (0 C).

Social Activities

There will be times when you get bored and lonely. Available activities sometimes will seem uninteresting or "cheesy." There are a multitude of activities you can explore, however, if you are open to trying new activities that you may have not previously thought of as social/recreational activities. You may find out that you enjoy hanging out with the local *babas* (grandmothers) and learning to can food, that you get used to spending hours on end at a local coffee shop (this is likely to be the most popular social activity in your town!), and that you are not comfortable spending much time at the local disco, as it may be full of your high school students. The trick is to find things that give you satisfaction and enjoyment. It is up to you to make the most of your leisure time, and there is plenty to do if you just look for it.

Bulgaria has museums, concerts, town festivals, theaters, athletic events, hot springs, outdoor markets, historical and ethnographic centers, coffee shops, bars, discos, and cinemas (in bigger towns and cities) for you to enjoy. The most recently released American films are shown in English with Bulgarian subtitles, but are usually dubbed by the time they make it to the video rental shops.

Bulgaria boasts some of the most magnificent natural areas in Eastern Europe, with a great diversity of flora and fauna. Opportunities for outdoor recreation include hiking, camping, rock climbing, and bird watching. Many of the towns in mountain regions have local hiking clubs. During the winter, Bulgarian ski resorts attract skiers from the United Kingdom, Germany, Russia, and the Nordic countries.

Professionalism, Dress, and Behavior

One of the difficulties of finding your place as a Peace Corps Volunteer is fitting into the local culture while maintaining your own cultural identity and being a professional all at the same time. It is not an easy thing to do successfully, and we can only provide you with guidelines. As a representative of a Bulgarian organization, you will be expected to dress and behave accordingly. "Business casual" is the catchall term for appropriate professional attire as a Volunteer in Bulgaria. You will be expected to dress as such throughout your pre-service training, and throughout your service as a Volunteer in Bulgaria.

Bulgarians dress very stylishly and take great pride in their appearance. They commonly, however, only have a few outfits that they wear repeatedly. While there is no hard-and-fast rule, a foreigner who wears ragged, torn or dirty clothing is likely to be considered disrespectful and possibly unreliable. Sloppy or overly casual attire can make it difficult to gain the respect and acceptance of your Bulgarian colleagues, particularly the older ones in positions of authority, whose support you will need to be successful. At the same time, Volunteers who out-dress the Bulgarians they work with may find they have difficulty fitting in. In general, Volunteers should dress to match their colleagues. Sometimes this can mean nice jeans and a casual, button-up shirt; other times this can mean wearing a tie daily. In an ethnic Bulgarian community, colorful and stylish attire is likely very appropriate, while in some minority communities, more modest dress is important. Keep in mind that you can purchase most clothing you would want for day-to-day use for reasonable prices throughout Bulgaria, so you may want to bring minimal clothing from the U.S. You will also have semiregular occasions to dress up for weddings and other special events, so bring some more formal attire in addition to professional clothes for everyday wear in the office or classroom. Casual clothes like jeans, shorts, T-shirts, and tank tops are also appropriate in some situations, but almost always outside of the professional environment. More casual printed T-shirts and baggy or old sweatshirts are typically used only for wear around the home and for sports activities, so you may find that newer looking solid colored T-shirts or fitted T-shirts (for women) are more versatile.

Personal Safety

More detailed information about the Peace Corps' approach to safety is contained in the Health Care and Safety chapter, but it is an important issue and cannot be overemphasized. As stated in the *Volunteer Handbook,* becoming a Peace Corps Volunteer entails certain safety risks. Living and traveling in an unfamiliar environment (oftentimes alone), having a limited understanding of local language and culture, and being perceived as well-off are some of the factors that can put a Volunteer at risk. Many Volunteers experience varying degrees of unwanted attention and harassment. Petty thefts and burglaries are not uncommon, and incidents of physical and sexual assault do occur, although most Bulgaria Volunteers complete their two years of service without personal security incidents. The Peace Corps has established procedures and policies designed to help you reduce your risks and enhance your safety and security. These procedures and policies, in addition to safety training, will be provided once you arrive in Bulgaria. At the same time, you are expected to take responsibility for your safety and well-being.

Each staff member at the Peace Corps is committed to providing Volunteers with the support they need to successfully meet the challenges they will face to have a safe, healthy, and productive service. We encourage Volunteers and families to look at our safety and security information on the Peace Corps website at www.peacecorps.gov/safety.

Information on these pages gives messages on Volunteer health and Volunteer safety. A video message from the Director is on this page, as well as a section titled "Safety and Security in Depth." This page lists topics ranging from the risks of serving as a Volunteer to posts' safety support systems to emergency planning and communications.

Rewards and Frustrations

Volunteers in Bulgaria must demonstrate a great deal of flexibility, patience, and maturity. You should expect frequent and lengthy delays in almost everything you are engaged in. Counterparts may sometimes feel threatened by your different methods, your energy, and your drive to work. When you first arrive at your site, you will need to focus on building relationships and gaining the trust of your colleagues and community. Then, you will be in a much stronger position to get things done. Many Volunteers find that once they are accepted by a community, they are "in" and are both embraced by their communities and are well-respected. It takes considerable time and effort to get to this point. Although earlier groups of Volunteers in Bulgaria have made the Peace Corps known to many communities, you may have to explain your role as a development worker. The concept of volunteerism is a bit odd to most Bulgarians. In spite of your modest stipend, you may be perceived as a rich foreigner. All Volunteers are expected to be highly motivated and proactive, flexible, professional, and committed to the Peace Corps' ideals and goals. The Peace Corps staff and current Volunteers take their commitment to serve the people of Bulgaria seriously. We invite you to join us in this effort, but only if you are confident that you can commit yourself to this challenging two-year assignment.

Because of the many economic and political difficulties and changes Bulgaria faces, the atmosphere in the country is one of uncertainty. The changes occurring in Bulgaria today are some of the most significant in its history, and Bulgarians from all walks of life are sacrificing time and comfort to make a new Bulgaria that is part of the global world. Being a part of this historic moment in Europe should be both fascinating and immensely satisfying to any Volunteer who is willing to work hard and give generously of his or her time.

PEACE CORPS TRAINING

Pre-Service Training

Pre-service training is the first event within a competency-based training program that continues throughout your 27 months of service in Bulgaria. Pre-service training ensures that Volunteers are equipped with the knowledge, skills, and attitudes to effectively perform their jobs. On average, nine of 10 trainees are sworn in as Volunteers.

Pre-service training is conducted in Bulgaria and directed by the Peace Corps with participation from representatives of Bulgaria organizations, former Volunteers, and/or training contractors. The length of pre-service training varies, usually ranging from 8-12 weeks, depending on the competencies required for the assignment. Bulgaria measures achievement of learning and determines if trainees have successfully achieved competencies, including language standards, for swearing in as a Peace Corps Volunteer.

Throughout service, Volunteers strive to achieve performance competencies. Initially, pre-service training affords the opportunity for trainees to develop and test their own resources. As a trainee, you will play an active role in self-education. You will be asked to decide how best to set and meet objectives and to find alternative solutions. You will be asked to prepare for an experience in which you will often have to take the initiative and accept responsibility for decisions. The success of your learning will be enhanced by your own effort to take responsibility for your learning and through sharing experiences with others.

Peace Corps training is founded on adult learning methods and often includes experiential "hands-on" applications such as conducting a participatory community needs assessment and facilitating groups. Successful training results in competence in various technical, linguistic, cross-cultural, health, and safety and security areas. Integrating into the community is usually one of the core competencies Volunteers strive to achieve both in pre-service training and during the first several months of service. Successful sustainable development work is based on the local trust and confidence Volunteers build by living in, and respectfully integrating into, the **Bulgarian** community and culture. Trainees are prepared for this through a "home-stay" experience, which often requires trainees to live with host families during pre-service training. Integration into the community not only facilitates good working relationships, but it fosters language learning and cross-cultural acceptance and trust, which help ensure your health, safety, and security.

Woven into the competencies, the ability to communicate in the host country language is critical to being an effective Peace Corps Volunteer. So basic is this precept that it is spelled out in the Peace Corps Act: No person shall be assigned to duty as a Volunteer under this act in any foreign country or area unless at the time of such assignment he (or she) possesses such reasonable proficiency as his (or her) assignment requires in speaking the language of the country or area to which he (or she) is assigned.

Qualifying for Service

The pre-service training experience provides an opportunity not only for the Peace Corps to assess a trainee's competence, but for trainees to re-evaluate their commitment to serve for 27 months to improve the quality of life of the people with whom Volunteers live and work and, in doing so, develop new knowledge, skills, and attitudes while adapting existing ones.

Peace Corps Bulgaria's competencies are designed to be accomplished throughout the Volunteer's 27 months of learning. A trainee may not be able to complete all learning objectives for a competency during pre-service training; however, he or she must show adequate progress toward achieving the competencies in order to become a Volunteer[1].

Bulgaria's competencies include the following:

Core Competencies:

1. **Integrate into local communities**

2. **Facilitate grassroots community development**

3. **Maintain personal health and safety to ensure effective service**

Education Sector Competencies:

1. Teach English as a foreign language to young and adult learners

2. Work effectively as a teacher in a Bulgarian school

3. Transfer skills, share experience and develop supplemental materials with Bulgarian teachers

COD Sector Competencies:

1. Support tourism development at grassroots level

---

[1] Peace Corps manual section 201.305.4.

2.   Help improve the ability of local organizations and businesses to facilitate local economic development

YD Sector Competencies:

1.   Help provide nonformal educational opportunities for disadvantaged and at-risk youth (including those with special needs, from orphanages and from ethnic minorities)

2.   Assist with tolerance building and better integration into society of disadvantaged youth (including those with special needs, from orphanages and from ethnic minorities)

3.   Help encourage institutional, parental, and community support for youth development efforts

Evaluation of your performance throughout service is a continual process, as Volunteers are responsible 24 hours a day, 7 days a week for personal conduct and professional performance. Successful completion of pre-service training is characterized by achievement of a set of learning objectives to determine competence. Failure to meet any of the selection standards by the completion of training may be grounds for a withdrawal of selection and disqualification from Peace Corps service.

Progress in one's own learning is a dialogue between you and the training staff. All of the training staff—including the training manager, and the language, technical, medical, safety and security, and cross-cultural trainers—will work with you toward the highest possible competencies by providing you with feedback on learning objective performance throughout training. After reviewing and observing your performance, the country director is responsible for making the final decision on whether you have qualified to serve as a Volunteer in the host country.

Upon successful completion of training, trainees who qualify for Peace Corps service are required by law to swear or affirm an oath of loyalty to the United States; it cannot be waived under any circumstances. The text of the oath is provided below. If you have any questions about the wording or meaning of the oath, consult a staff member during training.

I, (your name), do solemnly swear (or affirm) that I will support and defend the Constitution of the United States of America against all enemies, domestic or foreign, that I take this obligation freely, and without any mental reservation or purpose of evasion, and that I will well and faithfully discharge my duties in the Peace Corps (so help me God).

Ongoing Learning

You are expected to improve your knowledge and skills in the areas of technical, language, cross-cultural, diversity, health, and safety throughout your service as a Volunteer. Training staff provide learning objectives during the 27-month continuum to help guide Volunteers throughout service. The manner in which you do this may be formal, through tutoring or workshops organized by the host government or in-country staff, or informally, through conversations and reading. Your learning will continue after you become a Volunteer, formally and through in-service training opportunities, specialized language or technical workshops, and a close-of-service workshop to help you evaluate your service and prepare for your return to the United States.

Formal opportunities for ongoing learning in Bulgaria include the following:

1. In-service training

2. Midservice conference

3. Project Design and Management Workshop

4. Language refresher workshops

5. Technical refresher workshops

6. Close-of-Service Conference

The number, length, and design of these trainings are adapted to country-specific needs and conditions. The key to the Peace Corps training system is that learning events are competency-based, designed, implemented, and evaluated cooperatively by the Peace Corps staff and Volunteers.

YOUR HEALTH CARE AND
SAFETY IN BULGARIA

The Peace Corps' highest priority is maintaining the good health and safety of every Volunteer. Peace Corps medical programs emphasize the preventive, rather than the curative, approach to disease. The Peace Corps in Bulgaria maintains a clinic with a full-time medical officer, who takes care of Volunteers' primary health care needs. Additional medical services, such as testing and basic treatment, are also available in Bulgaria at local hospitals. If you become seriously ill, you will be transported either to an American-standard medical facility in the region or to the United States.

Health Issues in Bulgaria

Bulgaria's history of heavy industrialization with poor pollution controls has left a legacy, particularly in air pollution. Although greater attention is being given to reducing industrial emissions, this is occurring gradually, and many of the reductions in pollution so far are due to shutdowns or slowdowns of factories. Much of the air pollution in urban areas comes from auto emissions and the use of soft coal for heating. Volunteers assigned to urban areas may experience moderate to severe air pollution comparable to pollution levels in Los Angeles, Denver, and Chicago. Although most Volunteers do not suffer health effects from Bulgaria's air pollution, those with severe allergies or asthma will not be placed in heavily polluted areas.

Additionally, Bulgaria has an older-style nuclear power plant. This plant, which is vital to the country's electric power supply, is monitored regularly by the International Atomic Energy Agency, and some of its systems and controls have recently been upgraded. No Volunteers are placed at sites close to the plant.

Heavy cigarette smoking takes place in most homes, cafes, and workplaces. Those who are very sensitive to cigarette smoke, or to air pollution in general, should carefully consider whether to accept an assignment in Bulgaria.

Helping You Stay Healthy

The Peace Corps will provide you with all the necessary inoculations, medications, and information to stay healthy. Upon your arrival in Bulgaria, you will receive a medical handbook. At the end of training, you will receive a medical kit with supplies to take care of mild illnesses and first aid needs. The contents of the kit are listed later in this chapter.

During pre-service training, you will have access to basic medical supplies through the medical officer. However, you will be responsible for your own supply of prescription drugs and any other specific medical supplies you require, as the Peace Corps will not order these items during training. Please bring a three-month supply of any prescription drugs you use, since they may not be available here and it may take several months for shipments to arrive.

You will have physicals at midservice and at the end of your service. If you develop a serious medical problem during your service, the medical officer in Bulgaria will consult with the Office of Medical Services in Washington, D.C. If it is determined that your condition cannot be treated in Bulgaria, you may be sent out of the country for further evaluation and care..

Maintaining Your Health

As a Volunteer, you must accept considerable responsibility for your own health. Proper precautions will significantly reduce your risk of serious illness or injury. The adage "An ounce of prevention ..." becomes extremely important in areas where diagnostic and treatment facilities are not up to the standards of the United States.

Many illnesses that afflict Volunteers worldwide are entirely preventable if proper food and water precautions are taken. These illnesses include food poisoning, parasitic infections, hepatitis A, dysentery, Guinea worms, tapeworms, and typhoid fever. Your medical officer will discuss specific standards for water and food preparation in Bulgaria during pre-service training.

Abstinence is the only certain choice for preventing infection with HIV and other sexually transmitted diseases. You are taking risks if you choose to be sexually active. To lessen risk, use a condom every time you have sex. Whether your partner is a host country citizen, a fellow Volunteer, or anyone else, do not assume this person is free of HIV/AIDS or other STDs. You will receive more information from the medical officer about this important issue.

Volunteers are expected to adhere to an effective means of birth control to prevent an unplanned pregnancy. Your medical officer can help you decide on the most appropriate method to suit your individual needs. Contraceptive methods are available without charge from the medical officer.

It is critical to your health that you promptly report to the medical office or other designated facility for scheduled immunizations, and that you let the medical officer know immediately of significant illnesses and injuries.

Women's Health Information

Pregnancy is treated in the same manner as other Volunteer health conditions that require medical attention but also have programmatic ramifications. The Peace Corps is responsible for determining the medical risk and the availability of appropriate medical care if the Volunteer remains in-country. Given the circumstances under which Volunteers live and work in Peace Corps countries, it is rare that the Peace Corps' medical and programmatic standards for continued service during pregnancy can be met.

If feminine hygiene products are not available for you to purchase on the local market, the Peace Corps medical officer in Bulgaria will provide them. If you require a specific product, please bring a three-month supply with you.

Your Peace Corps Medical Kit

The Peace Corps medical officer will provide you with a kit that contains basic items necessary to prevent and treat illnesses that may occur during service. Kit items can be periodically restocked at the medical office.

Medical Kit Contents

Ace bandages

Adhesive tape

American Red Cross First Aid & Safety Handbook

Antacid tablets (Tums)

Antibiotic ointment (Bacitracin/Neomycin/Polymycin B)

Antiseptic antimicrobial skin cleaner (Hibiclens)

Band-Aids

Butterfly closures

Calamine lotion

Cepacol lozenges

Condoms

Dental floss

Diphenhydramine HCL 25 mg (Benadryl)

Insect repellent stick (Cutter's)

Iodine tablets (for water purification)

Lip balm (Chapstick)

Oral rehydration salts

Oral thermometer (Fahrenheit)

Pseudoephedrine HCL 30 mg (Sudafed)

Robitussin-DM lozenges (for cough)

Scissors

Sterile gauze pads

Tetrahydrozaline eyedrops (Visine)

Tinactin (antifungal cream)

Tweezers

Before You Leave: A Medical Checklist

If there has been any change in your health—physical, mental, or dental—since you submitted your examination reports to the Peace Corps, you must immediately notify the Office of Medical Services. Failure to disclose new illnesses, injuries, allergies, or pregnancy can endanger your health and may jeopardize your eligibility to serve.

If your dental exam was done more than a year ago, or if your physical exam is more than two years old, contact the Office of Medical Services to find out whether you need to update your records. If your dentist or Peace Corps dental consultant has recommended that you undergo dental treatment or repair, you must complete that work and make sure your dentist sends requested confirmation reports or X-rays to the Office of Medical Services.

If you wish to avoid having duplicate vaccinations, contact your physician's office to obtain a copy of your immunization record and bring it to your pre-departure orientation. If you have any immunizations prior to Peace Corps service, the Peace Corps cannot reimburse you for the cost. The Peace Corps will provide all the immunizations necessary for your overseas assignment, either at your pre-departure orientation or shortly after you arrive in Bulgaria. You do not need to begin taking malaria medication prior to departure.

Bring a three-month supply of any prescription or over-the-counter medication you use on a regular basis, including birth control pills. Although the Peace Corps cannot reimburse you for this three-month supply, it will order refills during your service. While awaiting shipment—which can take several months—you will be dependent on your own medication supply. The Peace Corps will not pay for herbal or nonprescribed medications, such as St. John's wort, glucosamine, selenium, or antioxidant supplements.

You are encouraged to bring copies of medical prescriptions signed by your physician. This is not a requirement, but they might come in handy if you are questioned in transit about carrying a three-month supply of prescription drugs.

If you wear eyeglasses, bring two pairs with you—a pair and a spare. If a pair breaks, the Peace Corps will replace it, using the information your doctor in the United States provided on the eyeglasses form during your examination. The Peace Corps discourages you from using contact lenses during your service to reduce your risk of developing a serious infection or other eye disease. Most Peace Corps countries do not have appropriate water and sanitation to support eye care with the use of contact lenses. The Peace Corps will not supply or replace contact lenses or associated solutions unless an ophthalmologist has recommended their use for a specific medical condition and the Peace Corps' Office of Medical Services has given approval.

If you are eligible for Medicare, are over 50 years of age, or have a health condition that may restrict your future participation in health care plans, you may wish to consult an insurance specialist about unique coverage needs before your departure. The Peace Corps will provide all necessary health care from the time you leave for your pre-departure orientation until you complete your service. When you finish, you will be entitled to the post-service health care benefits described in the Peace Corps *Volunteer Handbook*. You may wish to consider keeping an existing health plan in effect during your service if you think age or preexisting conditions might prevent you from reenrolling in your current plan when you return home.

Safety and Security—Our Partnership

Serving as a Volunteer overseas entails certain safety and security risks. Living and traveling in an unfamiliar environment, a limited understanding of the local language and culture, and the perception of being a wealthy American are some of the factors that can put a Volunteer at risk. Property theft and burglaries are not uncommon. Incidents of physical and sexual assault do occur, although almost all Volunteers complete their two years of service without serious personal safety problems.

Beyond knowing that Peace Corps approaches safety and security as a partnership with you, it might be helpful to see how this partnership works. The Peace Corps has policies, procedures, and training in place to promote your safety. We depend on you to follow those policies and to put into practice what you have learned. An example of how this works in practice—in this case to help manage the risk of burglary—is:

- Peace Corps assesses the security environment where you will live and work
- Peace Corps inspects the house where you will live according to established security criteria
- Peace Corp provides you with resources to take measures such as installing new locks
- Peace Corps ensures you are welcomed by host country authorities in your new community
- Peace Corps responds to security concerns that you raise
- You lock your doors and windows
- You adopt a lifestyle appropriate to the community where you live
- You get to know neighbors
- You decide if purchasing personal articles insurance is appropriate for you
- You don't change residences before being authorized by Peace Corps
- You communicate concerns that you have to Peace Corps staff.

This *Welcome Book* contains sections on: Living Conditions and Volunteer Lifestyle; Peace Corps Training; and Your Health Care and Safety that all include important safety and security information to help you understand this partnership. The Peace Corps makes every effort to give Volunteers the tools they need to function in the safest way possible, because working to maximize the safety and security of Volunteers is our highest priority. Not only do we provide you with training and tools to prepare for the unexpected, but we teach you to identify, reduce, and manage the risks you may encounter.

Factors that Contribute to Volunteer Risk

There are several factors that can heighten a Volunteer's risk, many of which are within the Volunteer's control. By far the most common crime that Volunteers experience are thefts. Thefts often occur when volunteers are away from their sites, in crowded locations (such as markets or on public transportation), and when leaving items unattended.

Before you depart for Bulgaria there are several measures you can take to recuce your risk:

- Leave valuable obbjects in the U.S.
- Leave copies of important documents and account numbers in the U.S. with someone you trust.
- Purchase a hidden money pouch or "dummy" wallet as a decoy
- Purchase personal articles insurance

After you arrive in Bulgaria, you will receive more detailed information about common crimes, factors that contribute to Volunteer risk, and local strategies to reduce that risk. For example, Volunteers in Bulgaria learn to:

- Choose safe routes and times for travel, and travel with someone trusted by the community whenever possible
- Make sure one's personal appearance is respectful of local customs
- Avoid high-crime areas
- Know the local language to get help in an emergency
- Make friends with local people who are respected in the community
- Limit alcohol consumption

As you can see from this list, you have to be willing to work hard and adapt your lifestyle to minimize the potential for being a target for crime. As with anywhere in the world, crime does exist in Bulgaria. You can reduce your risk by avoiding situations that place you at risk and by taking precautions. Crime at the village or town level is less frequent than in large cities; people know each other and generally are less likely to steal from their neighbors. Tourist attractions in large towns are favorite worksites for pickpockets.

The following are other security concerns in Bulgaria of which you should be aware:

Bulgaria is a relatively safe place to live from the standpoint of personal security. However, it is not without petty crimes and assaults. Do not let yourself be lulled into a false sense of security. If you follow a few simple guidelines, you can make a relatively safe place even safer.

Avoid dangerous places. Before you wander off alone, make inquiries. Make local friends and contacts; they will be the best source for this kind of information. Try to stay out of underpasses and don't linger in train stations. Do not carry valuables or important documents in your backpack. Make sure that you secure your valuables: lock your house and bicycle if you have one, keep your valuables in a hidden place (and remember where), and obtain personal articles insurance so you can replace valuable items if a theft does occur.

Historically, transportation accidents have presented the greatest risks to the safety of trainees and Volunteers. Because the transportation systems available present specific challenges and hazards, Peace Corps/Bulgaria has developed a country specific transportation policy in order to minimize the risks associated with travel. In every case trainees and Volunteers are strongly advised to choose the safest transportation option available and should travel at times and on routes that present the lowest risk.

Volunteers tend to attract a lot of attention both in large cities and at their sites, but they are more likely to receive negative attention in highly populated centers, and away from their support network —friends and colleagues—who look out for them. While whistles and exclamations may be fairly common on the street, this behavior can be reduced if you dress conservatively, abide by local cultural norms, and respond according to the training you will receive.

Volunteers tend to attract a lot of attention both in large cities and at their sites, but they are more likely to receive negative attention in highly populated centers, and away from their support network —friends and colleagues—who look out for them. While whistles and exclamations may be fairly common on the street, this behavior can be reduced if you dress conservatively, abide by local cultural norms, and respond according to the training you will receive.

Staying Safe: Don't Be a Target for Crime

You must be prepared to take on a large degree of responsibility for your own safety. You can make yourself less of a target, ensure that your home is secure, and develop relationships in your community that will make you an unlikely victim of crime. While the factors that contribute to your risk in Bulgaria may be different, in many ways you can better assure your safety by doing what you would do if you moved to a new city anywhere: Be cautious, check things out, ask questions, learn about your neighborhood, know where the more risky locations are, use common sense, and be aware. You can reduce your vulnerability to crime by integrating into your community, learning the local language, acting responsibly, and abiding by Peace Corps policies and procedures. Serving safely and effectively in Bulgaria will require that you accept some restrictions on your current lifestyle.

Support from Staff

If a trainee or Volunteer is the victim of a safety incident, Peace Corps staff is prepared to provide support. All Peace Corps posts have procedures in place to respond to incidents of crime committed against Volunteers. The first priority for all posts in the aftermath of an incident is to ensure the Volunteer is safe and receiving medical treatment as needed. After assuring the safety of the Volunteer, Peace Corps staff members provide support by reassessing the Volunteer's worksite and housing arrangements and making any adjustments, as needed. In some cases, the nature of the incident may necessitate a site or housing transfer. Peace Corps staff will also assist Volunteers with preserving their rights to pursue legal sanctions against the perpetrators of the crime. It is very important that Volunteers report incidents as they occur, not only to protect their peer Volunteers, but also to preserve the future right to prosecute. Should Volunteers decide later in the process that they want to proceed with the prosecution of their assailant, this option may no longer exist if the evidence of the event has not been preserved at the time of the incident.

Crime Data for Bulgaria

The country-specific data chart below shows the average annual rates of major types of crimes reported by Peace Corps Volunteers/trainees in **Bulgaria** compared to all other Europe, Mediterranean and Asia programs as a whole. It can be understood as an approximation of the number of reported incidents per 100 Volunteers in a year[2].

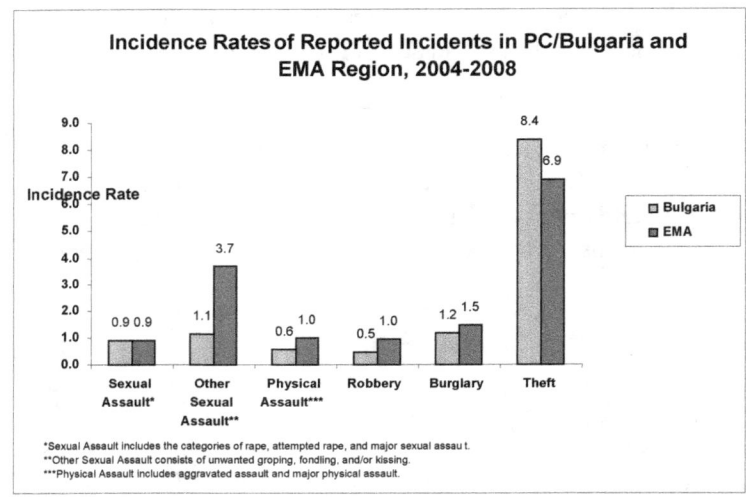

Few Peace Corps Volunteers are victims of serious crimes and crimes that do occur overseas are investigated and prosecuted by local authorities through the local courts system. If you are the victim of a crime, you will decide if you wish to pursue prosecution. If you decide to prosecute, Peace Corps will be there to assist you. One of our tasks

---

[2] The incidence rate for each type of crime is the number of crime events relative to the Volunteer/trainee population. It is expressed on the chart as a ratio of crime to Volunteer and trainee years (or V/T years, which is a measure of 12 full months of V/T service) to allow for a statistically valid way to compare crime data across countries.

is to ensure you are fully informed of your options and understand how the local legal process works. Peace Corps will help you ensure your rights are protected to the fullest extent possible under the laws of the country.

If you are the victim of a serious crime, you will learn how to get to a safe location as quickly as possible and contact your Peace Corps office. It's important that you notify Peace Corps as soon as you can so Peace Corps can provide you with the help you need.

Volunteer Safety Support in Bulgaria

The Peace Corps' approach to safety is a five-pronged plan to help you stay safe during your service and includes the following: information sharing, Volunteer training, site selection criteria, a detailed emergency action plan, and protocols for addressing safety and security incidents. Bulgaria's in-country safety program is outlined below.

The Peace Corps/Bulgaria office will keep you informed of any issues that may impact Volunteer safety through **information sharing**. Regular updates will be provided in Volunteer newsletters and in memorandums from the country director. In the event of a critical situation or emergency, you will be contacted through the emergency communication network. An important component of the capacity of the Peace Corps to keep you informed is your buy-in to the partnership concept with the Peace Corps staff. It is expected that you will do your part in ensuring that Peace Corps staff members are kept apprised of your movements in-country so that they are capable of informing you.

Volunteer training will include sessions on specific safety and security issues in Bulgaria. This training will prepare you to adopt a culturally appropriate lifestyle and exercise judgment that promotes safety and reduces risk in your home, at work, and while traveling. Safety training is offered throughout service and is integrated into the language, cross-cultural aspects, health, and other components of training. You will be expected to successfully complete all training competencies in a variety of areas, including safety and security, as a condition of service.

Certain **site selection criteria** are used to determine safe housing for Volunteers before their arrival. The Peace Corps staff works closely with host communities and counterpart agencies to help prepare them for a Volunteer's arrival and to establish expectations of their respective roles in supporting the Volunteer. Each site is inspected before the Volunteer's arrival to ensure placement in appropriate, safe, and secure housing and worksites. Site selection is based, in part, on any relevant site history; access to medical, banking, postal, and other essential services; availability of communications, transportation, and markets; different housing options and living arrangements; and other Volunteer support needs.

You will also learn about Peace Corps/Bulgaria's **detailed emergency action plan**, which is implemented in the event of civil or political unrest or a natural disaster. When you arrive at your site, you will complete and submit a site locator form with your address, contact information, and a map to your house. If there is a security threat, you will gather with other Volunteers in Bulgaria at predetermined locations until the situation is resolved or the Peace Corps decides to evacuate.

Finally, in order for the Peace Corps to be fully responsive to the needs of Volunteers, it is imperative that Volunteers immediately report any security incident to the Peace Corps office. The Peace Corps has established protocols for **addressing safety and security incidents** in a timely and appropriate manner, and it collects and evaluates safety and security data to track trends and develop strategies to minimize risks to future Volunteers.

DIVERSITY AND CROSS-CULTURAL ISSUES

In fulfilling its mandate to share the face of America with host countries, the Peace Corps is making special efforts to see that all of America's richness is reflected in the Volunteer corps. More Americans of color are serving in today's Peace Corps than at any time in recent years. Differences in race, ethnic background, age, religion, and sexual orientation are expected and welcomed among our Volunteers. Part of the Peace Corps' mission is to help dispel any notion that Americans are all of one origin or race and to establish that each of us is as thoroughly American as the other despite our many differences.

Our diversity helps us accomplish that goal. In other ways, however, it poses challenges. In Bulgaria, as in other Peace Corps host countries, Volunteers' behavior, lifestyle, background, and beliefs are judged in a cultural context very different from their own. Certain personal perspectives or characteristics commonly accepted in the United States may be quite uncommon, unacceptable, or even repressed in Bulgaria.

Outside of Bulgaria's capital, residents of rural communities have had relatively little direct exposure to other cultures, races, religions, and lifestyles. What people view as typical American behavior or norms may be a misconception, such as the belief that all Americans are rich and have blond hair and blue eyes. The people of Bulgaria are justly known for their generous hospitality to foreigners; however, members of the community in which you will live may display a range of reactions to cultural differences that you present.

To ease the transition and adapt to life in Bulgaria, you may need to make some temporary, yet fundamental compromises in how you present yourself as an American and as an individual. For example, female trainees and Volunteers may not be able to exercise the independence available to them in the United States; political discussions need to be handled with great care; and some of your personal beliefs may best remain undisclosed. You will need to develop techniques and personal strategies for coping with these and other limitations. The Peace Corps staff will lead diversity and sensitivity discussions during pre-service training and will be on call to provide support, but the challenge ultimately will be your own.

Overview of Diversity in Bulgaria

The Peace Corps staff in Bulgaria recognizes the adjustment issues that come with diversity and will endeavor to provide support and guidance. During pre-service training, several sessions will be held to discuss diversity and coping mechanisms. We look forward to having male and female Volunteers from a variety of races, ethnic groups, ages, religions, and sexual orientations, and hope that you will become part of a diverse group of Americans who take pride in supporting one another and demonstrating the richness of American culture.

What Might a Volunteer Face?

Possible Issues for Female Volunteers

Bulgaria has been working to align its laws with the requirements of the European Union, which it joined in January 2007. Yet legislation to protect women against sexual harassment and discrimination has only recently been introduced.

As with any other social matter, there is a large difference in attitudes toward gender between smaller communities and big cities and between the older and younger generations. Traditionally, especially in more rural areas, Bulgarian women are expected to cook and look after other needs of their husbands and children while they also hold jobs outside of the home. In turn, women often expect men to open doors for them, to give them their seats on public transportation, and to show them other signs of courtesy. Women also often expect men to help if they are performing a task that is considered difficult or demeaning, and men will offer to help women whom they believe are confused by minor mechanical or equipment-related problems. Female Volunteers may, therefore, feel their skills are questioned in the typically male professional environment. Another common occurrence is for young women to be honked at by drivers or yelled at by groups of young men in the streets. If this happens to you, it is best to ignore the behavior and avoid making eye contact, as any response is likely to aggravate the situation.

Possible Issues for Volunteers of Color

You may be the only minority trainee or Volunteer within a particular project. You may not receive, or be able to receive, the type of personal support you want from other Volunteers. While staff and your fellow Volunteers will do their very best to support you, there may not be current Volunteers or staff role models who can personally relate to your experiences.

Once you move to your site, you are likely to live among people who have no experience or understanding of a non-Caucasian-American culture. Because of ignorance, stereotypes, cultural perceptions, or Bulgaria's historical involvement with certain countries, you are likely to encounter varying degrees of harassment in your day-to-day life. Most commonly, you may not be perceived as being American. In any community where you are not known, you need to be prepared for staring, pointing, and comments, often mostly because people find you interesting. Finally, you should be prepared to hear derogatory terms and racial comments that would be completely inappropriate in the United States. Such offensive terms usually are uttered because people are not aware of acceptable terms in English, and instances where the intent is to harass or offend are infrequent. Bulgarians as a whole tend to be very accepting, curious, and open to individuals once they get to know them on a personal level. Many Volunteers of color have been extremely well accepted and well liked in their communities, once their communities came to know and accept them, and once they become more comfortable with higher levels of attention when they travel outside of their communities. Their time in Bulgarian communities has had a significant and positive impact on how the community members understand and appreciate diversity.

Peace Corps/Bulgaria currently has African Americans, Arab Americans, Asian Americans, Hispanic Americans, and other members of minority groups among its Volunteer corps. They all manage these issues in their own way. Members of the Peace Corps staff will do everything they can to help you work through any challenges.

Possible Issues for Senior Volunteers

Overall, senior Volunteers are highly valued for the wealth of experience they bring to their communities and counterparts. Yet you may sometimes feel isolated within the Peace Corps community because most Volunteers are in their 20s. They may have little understanding of, or respect for, the lives and experiences of senior Americans. You may also find that while younger Volunteers cannot always offer you support, they still look to you for advice and support. While some seniors find this a very enjoyable part of their Volunteer experience, others choose not to fill this role.

Training may present its own special challenges. Older trainees have sometimes found that the learning environment does not completely match the learning style and material they are most comfortable with in terms of timing, presentation of materials, comfort level, and health. You may need to be assertive in developing an effective individual approach to language learning. And, when possible, you may need to collaborate on identifying sites and assignments most appropriate for an older Volunteer. Peace Corps staff members have much experience supporting and mentoring Volunteers of all ages and are here to support you.

Before leaving for Bulgaria, you should consider how you will deal with issues such as possible family emergencies, maintaining lifelong friendships, and deciding who will have Power of Attorney for attending to your financial matters

Possible Issues for Gay, Lesbian, or Bisexual Volunteers

In general, Bulgarians view homosexuality as immoral. There are, of course, many Bulgarians with alternative lifestyles, but their lifestyle would not be well accepted in Bulgaria if they chose to be open about it. Most Bulgarians choose to keep their personal lifestyles private, and there seems to be an attitude of acceptance when a community does not need to acknowledge a person's sexual preference. Almost all GLBT Peace Corps/Bulgaria Volunteers find that they cannot be open about their sexual preference in their assigned communities, although some find a few close Bulgarian friends that they can confide in. Most GLBT Volunteers find that they can be open with Peace Corps/Bulgaria staff and Volunteers, and find the Peace Corps community to be a source of significant support.

Relationships with host country nationals can happen, but they may not be easy. Lesbians, like all American women, are likely to have to deal with constant questions about boyfriends, marriage, and sex. Wearing an "engagement ring" may help. Gay (and straight) men may have to deal with machismo while with Bulgarian males, including talk of sexual conquests, girl watching, and dirty jokes. Volunteers with alternative lifestyles have occasionally set up informal forums for support and information sharing.

Possible Religious Issues for Volunteers

The Bulgarian Orthodox Church is the dominant religion (official statistics report that 83 percent of Bulgarians consider themselves members), so you may not be able to find an active Protestant, Catholic, Jewish, or Muslim congregation near your site and may need to travel to a bigger city to attend religious events or ceremonies. Only Christmas and Easter are observed as official religious holidays. Alternatively, you could be living in a primarily Muslim community, and only Muslim religious services may be easily accessible.

As in most countries, there are some people who hold stereotypes about members of other faiths. Volunteers have reported being asked about their religion and not always getting a positive response. Some Volunteers say they try to avoid discussion of religious beliefs. In general, Bulgarians are not an overly religious people, but Bulgarian culture and religious heritage go hand-in-hand for many Bulgarians. Peace Corps/Bulgaria has Volunteers of many faiths, and most of them find that the question of religion does not interfere with the work they are doing in Bulgaria or the friendships they form.

Possible Issues for Volunteers With Disabilities

As part of the medical clearance process, the Peace Corps Office of Medical Services determined that you were physically and emotionally capable, with or without reasonable accommodations, to perform a full tour of Volunteer service in **Bulgaria** without unreasonable risk of harm to yourself or interruption of service. The Peace Corps/ **Bulgaria** staff will work with disabled Volunteers to make reasonable accommodations for them in training, housing, job sites, or other areas to enable them to serve safely and effectively.

As a Volunteer with a disability in Bulgaria, you may face a special set of challenges. Bulgaria has an old, poorly maintained infrastructure that does not always accommodate individuals with disabilities. Few public places, for example, have been made accessible to wheelchairs. Because sidewalks are uneven and cars frequently park in pedestrian areas, visually impaired Volunteers may have a harder time moving around on their own

Possible Issues for Married Volunteers

Married couples should expect to live separately during their pre-service training. Typically, married trainees in Bulgaria, particularly those working in the same Peace Corps sector, live with separate host families in the same community during their pre-service training, and attend language classes together daily. Most Peace Corps couples report that the advantages—more opportunities to speak Bulgarian during the host family stay, more opportunities to have their own host family experience—are well worth the challenges of living apart during this time. Occasionally, couples have had to live in separate communities during pre-service training when they are in different program sectors (YD, COD, and TEFL). Peace Corps/Bulgaria will make reasonable efforts to take proximity into account and to support some visitation for married couples during training. All married couples will live together as Volunteers at their permanent sites after they finish pre-service training and swear in as Volunteers.

Married couples may face challenges stemming from traditional Bulgarian gender roles. A married female Volunteer may find herself the object of gossip among older Bulgarian women, who may wonder whether she is taking proper care of her husband, can cook and preserve enough vegetables for the winter, or spends too much time with other men. While the wife may be expected to do all the domestic chores, the husband may be expected to assume an overtly dominant role in the household. In addition, the independence exercised by each member of an American couple may be perceived as immoral behavior in more conservative communities. Most married couples, however, have served successfully in Bulgaria without making unreasonable compromises.

FREQUENTLY ASKED QUESTIONS

How much luggage am I allowed to bring to Bulgaria?
Most airlines have baggage size and weight limits and assess charges for transport of baggage that exceeds those limits. The Peace Corps has its own size and weight limits and will not pay the cost of transport for baggage that exceeds these limits. The Peace Corps' allowance is two checked pieces of luggage with combined dimensions of both pieces not to exceed 107 inches (length + width + height) and a carry-on bag with dimensions of no more than 45 inches. Checked baggage should not exceed 80 pounds [or 100 for countries with cold weather] total with a maximum weight of 50 pounds for any one bag.

Peace Corps Volunteers are not allowed to take pets, weapons, explosives, radio transmitters (shortwave radios are permitted), automobiles, or motorcycles to their overseas assignments. Do not pack flammable materials or liquids such as lighter fluid, cleaning solvents, hair spray, or aerosol containers. This is an important safety precaution.

What is the electric current in Bulgaria?
220 V

How much money should I bring?
Volunteers are expected to live at the same level as the people in their community. You will be given a settling-in allowance and a monthly living allowance, which should cover your expenses. Often Volunteers wish to bring additional money for vacation travel to other countries. Credit cards and traveler's checks are preferable to cash. If you choose to bring extra money, bring the amount that will suit your own travel plans and needs.

When can I take vacation and have people visit me?
Each Volunteer accrues two vacation days per month of service (excluding training). Leave may not be taken during training, the first three months of service, or the last three months of service, except in conjunction with an authorized emergency leave. Family and friends are welcome to visit you after pre-service training and the first three months of service as long as their stay does not interfere with your work. Extended stays at your site are not encouraged and may require permission from your country director. The Peace Corps is not able to provide your visitors with visa, medical, or travel assistance.

Will my belongings be covered by insurance?
The Peace Corps does not provide insurance coverage for personal effects; Volunteers are ultimately responsible for the safekeeping of their personal belongings. However, you can purchase personal property insurance before you leave. If you wish, you may contact your own insurance company; additionally, insurance application forms will be provided, and we encourage you to consider them carefully. Volunteers should not ship or take valuable items

overseas. Jewelry, watches, radios, cameras, and expensive appliances are subject to loss, theft, and breakage, and in many places, satisfactory maintenance and repair services are not available.

Do I need an international driver's license?

Volunteers in Bulgaria do not need an international driver's license because they are prohibited from operating privately owned motorized vehicles. Most urban travel is by bus or taxi. Rural travel ranges from buses and minibuses to trucks, bicycles, and lots of walking. On very rare occasions, a Volunteer may be asked to drive a sponsor's vehicle, but this can occur only with prior written permission of the country director. Should this occur, the Volunteer may obtain a local driver's license. A U.S. driver's license will facilitate the process, so bring it with you just in case.

What should I bring as gifts for Bulgarian friends and my host family?

This is not a requirement. A token of friendship is sufficient. Some gift suggestions include knickknacks for the house; pictures, books, or calendars of American scenes; souvenirs from your area; hard candies that will not melt or spoil; or photos to give away.

Where will my site assignment be when I finish training and how isolated will I be?

Peace Corps trainees are not assigned to individual sites until after they have completed pre-service training. This gives Peace Corps staff the opportunity to assess each trainee's technical and language skills prior to assigning sites, in addition to finalizing site selections with their ministry counterparts. If feasible, you may have the opportunity to provide input on your site preferences, including geographical location, distance from other Volunteers, and living conditions. However, keep in mind that many factors influence the site selection process and that the Peace Corps cannot guarantee placement where you would ideally like to be. Most Volunteers live in small towns or in rural villages and are usually within one hour from another Volunteer. Some sites require a 10-to-12-hour drive from the capital. There is at least one Volunteer based in each of the regional capitals and about five to eight Volunteers in the capital city.

How can my family contact me in an emergency?

The Peace Corps' Office of Special Services provides assistance in handling emergencies affecting trainees and Volunteers or their families. Before leaving the United States, instruct your family to notify the Office of Special Services immediately if an emergency arises, such as a serious illness or death of a family member. During normal business hours, the number for the Office of Special Services is 800.424.8580; select option 2, then extension 1470. After normal business hours and on weekends and holidays, the Special Services duty officer can be reached at the above number. For nonemergency questions, your family can get information from your country desk staff at the Peace Corps by calling 800.424.8580.

Can I call home from Bulgaria?

You will not have quick or easy access to a telephone when you first arrive in Bulgaria. Advise family and friends that it could be several weeks after your arrival in Bulgaria before you have the time or opportunity to call home. This situation may change after you purchase a cellphone and determine the best options for Internet access available to you.

Standard long-distance telephone service is available but expensive. If you are calling on a landline from outside the capital, it may take a while to get a connection. Some calling cards from the United States (e.g., those issued by AT&T, MCI, and Sprint) can be used to call the United States. However, you cannot use these cards to call from Bulgaria to other countries because of a phone block in Bulgaria. There are multiple alternate providers that offer calls for just a few cents per minute from the U.S. to Bulgaria and only from Sofia and a few other major cities in Bulgaria to the U.S., including Foneca and others.

Most Volunteers who have home Internet access and a laptop use Skype or VoIPStunt to call to the U.S. Those who don't, tend to call from an Internet club in their village or a nearby town or have family and friends in the U.S. call them. You alternatively can make international calls from a local public telephone or post office. The country code for Bulgaria is 359.

Should I bring a cellular phone with me?

It is not recommended. Peace Corps/Bulgaria will provide you with adequate funds and instructions to purchase a cellphone locally. Cellphones and cellphone plans are much cheaper in Bulgaria than in the United States. Often, with the purchase of a plan the phone will be free or at a very reduced cost

Should I bring my computer? Will there be email and Internet access?

Internet and email access is becoming more available, and Internet cafes can be found in most major cities and towns. Many small villages, however, do not have Internet access. Many Volunteers bring laptops with them, and are happy they have them, but many other Volunteers do fine without them. If you bring a computer, you should purchase personal property insurance for the computer and other valuables before you leave; it is not that expensive and well worth the price. The Peace Corps does not provide this coverage.

WELCOME LETTERS FROM BULGARIA VOLUNTEERS

Greetings from Bulgaria,

I imagine at the moment you are excited, nervous, and more than a bit curious about the next two years of your lives. Many of you will be living in small villages. Living in a village offers a number of challenges which are, without a doubt, outweighed by the rewards.

The most obvious challenges, but in fact the easiest to deal with, will be material. You will have to cope with some or all of the following inconveniences: limited or no Internet access, regular power outages, water shortages, limited bus access to and from the village, and the joys of trying to stay warm with a wood stove in the winter. During the past two years working as a teacher, I have learned that the obvious challenges are quickly forgotten while the real challenges are less tangible and more job-related. Many of your students will have little or no experience with computers. Most of your co-workers will be farmers and will divide their time between the two jobs, often giving more attention to the latter, depending on the season. If you are in a minority community, many of your students will not be proficient in Bulgarian language. Whatever challenges you face, it's important to remember that challenges open up opportunities for solutions, in which you will play a part.

Bulgarians, especially in the villages, are famous for their hospitality. My co-workers and neighbors feel personally responsible for my well-being. This manifests itself primarily through appeals to my stomach. As a teacher I am a respected member of the community, which allows me to effectively fill the role of a change agent. The sense of community and the openness with which people have invited me to be part of their lives has motivated me and made this experience meaningful.

Learning the language is the key to living and working in a foreign country. People are much more inclined to sit down with me and share their lives because they know I am able to share my opinions in an intelligible way. It would be very difficult to work with the students and with my co-workers if we could not communicate effectively. Besides learning the language, the only other piece of advice I can offer is the importance of being flexible. Let your circumstances shape your expectations and work tirelessly to accomplish as much as possible.

You are about to take on a service that will mean a lot to many people. I can guarantee that you will get as much out of your experience here as you put into it.

Good luck!

— *English Teacher (TEFL)*

Life in Bulgaria can be confusing, exciting, intensive, relaxing, and enlightening all at the same time. A day feels like eternity but two years feels like a day. When I came to Bulgaria I expected crowded smelly buses, less than ideal customer service, small town gossip, and weird stares. What I did not expect was to stand out because I am African American.

The first few weeks I was at my permanent site I noticed people would hang out of their car windows to get a better look at me. Some people went as far as to yell the "N" word or "Black Monkey" as if they did not want me here. I felt insulted and hurt because I had traveled so far from my family to come. I felt ill prepared; no one told me I would encounter people that were not tolerant of racial differences. The hardest part of my service was adjusting to this aspect of Bulgarian culture.

Two years later I still stand out; however, now I understand the reason why. Most Bulgarians did not have contact with people from different cultures until the fall of communism in 1989. I got the full understanding of how I must look to Bulgarians after I saw black people in my town for the first time. They really stood out and I was drawn to them. I shouted for them to turn around, but they kept walking. I began to wave my hands and screamed louder to get their attention, but they ignored me. I realized at that moment I was treating them the same way Bulgarians treated me! It clicked that people were simply interested in me because I am different.

I extended and stayed an additional year because, looking over my first two years, the positive experiences outweighed the negative experiences. I could not let a few people and situations stop me from accomplishing my goals of volunteering with the Peace Corps. I had to change my attitude to focus on the positive things rather than the negative. I have tons of friends who love and care about me in Bulgaria. I cannot imagine having served anywhere else in the world.

—*Crystal H. Brown, B20 Community and Organizational Development*

Hi there,

If you are reading this letter, it means you have made it through the tedious application process, and have chosen to serve as a Peace Corps Volunteer for 27 months in Bulgaria. That's no small feat and quite a privilege that has been extended to you. So, congratulations on your decision; it won't be easy, but for my wife and me, it has been an incredible experience and one of the best decisions of our lives.

Your in-country experience will start with literally a world-class language, technical, and cultural training course while living with a host family and getting your first glimpse of this rich and complex culture steeped in history, tradition, ritual, and even a little superstition. Throughout your two years of service, as you continue to receive training, support, and guidance from the incredibly talented and dedicated staff, you will also have the opportunity to delve deeper into this truly amazing place.

As a married couple joining the Peace Corps, we were not sure what to expect. We knew we would be in a small minority, with just one or two other couples per group. And, we knew our experience would be a bit different. We wouldn't be living together under the same roof during the three months of training, but we would have a built-in support system between the two of us, for those days when nothing seemed to work in our favor. Though it wasn't easy living apart for those initial three months, it turned out to be a great opportunity. It was an opportunity to have two host families instead of one, which forced us to immerse ourselves in this new language and culture much more so than if we had lived together.

Being married Volunteers here in Bulgaria has meant double the friends, double the activities, and double the opportunities to serve the Peace Corps mission. It also meant being accepted into Bulgarian society in a different way, as it was easier for many of our new friends and acquaintances to understand and relate to us, since we were a *semeistvo* (family). But we didn't do everything together; we also had our separate primary and secondary assignments, based on our individual skill sets and our personal interests. We each got to exercise our own strengths at our respective workplaces, all while sharing the experience of teaching English once in a while and putting together a summer camp for kids.

Regarding packing, we will share only two pieces of advice: bring all the patience you have, and try to leave your expectations at home. You can get everything else here. Every bit of effort put into learning the language before you arrive and every day that you are here will make your stay more fruitful and rewarding and make the process of integration much more fluid.

Have a wonderful time in this beautiful country, rich with history, culture, nature, and some of the most hospitable people on earth. And, be thankful you have been extended the chance to become part of the legacy that is Peace Corps/Bulgaria.

-Brian Fassett, B16 Community and Organizational Development, and Kate Fassett, B16 Youth Development

Greetings! You are about to come to a place that is impossible to describe in only a few words. In Bulgaria, laundry on the line fights for space with satellite dishes on the balconies of the ubiquitous communist-era block apartments. One walks to school past an old woman wearing a scarf, herding her goats, contrasted with teenage girls wearing platform shoes and trendy zigzag parts in their hair. The Backstreet Boys are on the radio in the background as families make homemade rakiya.

Cellphones are everywhere, but people still go to city parks to collect chestnuts for the winter and for home remedies. Why does a good bottle of wine cost less than a can of tuna? Why is it bad luck to sit at the corner of a table or to place your bread loaf upside down? You'll discover the answers to these questions and much more. If you're a teacher, be prepared to wrestle with tough educational issues, such as teaching to multilevel classes and teaching with minimal supplies and materials.

What to bring? Bring small gifts for your host family, such as nice paper napkins with interesting designs, general-interest magazines with lots of pictures, and packaged foods that are specific to the United States or your region (such as wild rice or dried cranberries). Bring photos of family and friends and postcards showing your hometown and state (especially in different seasons). Bulgarians are very curious about life in the United States. Many of them think it's exactly like what they see on "Baywatch" and "Dynasty". It's good to give them a more accurate picture.

As a teacher, I'm happy I brought my laptop, thick markers, and colorful alphabet cards to post. I wish I had brought stickers (with English expressions like "Fantastic!" and "Super!"). Bring professional-looking clothes that are easy to maintain (hand-washable, in dark colors). Business-casual mix-and-match items seem the best for crossover from professional to hiking and leisure. Bring sandals, nice shoes, and boots that look good but are practical for walking everywhere. You can have things sent from home, but receiving packages can be dicey, so bring the more valuable and bulky belongings with you. The most important thing: Bring flexibility and an open mind. You'll be frustrated at times by your lack of ability to express yourself or be listened to. For example, I have yet to meet a host mother who acknowledges the phrase, "No thank you, I'm full."

You will be surprised at what you miss about America and sometimes exasperated by what you might perceive as backward or defeatist thinking, but it's fascinating to discover who these people are and how they've come to be this way. You are likely to realize that you are learning more than you are teaching.

—*English Teacher (TEFL)*

I was watching an interview on CNN about the recently passed Egyptian director Youssef Chahine, and one of his protégés made a comment about him that stayed with me. He said that success is a combination of talent, skill, and luck. I really like true statements and I think that it's very true about my Peace Corps service as a youth development Volunteer.

I have been working almost daily in a community center and nongovernmental organization for Roma and Bulgarian youth. I have done a lot of successful projects as a Volunteer, and not one of them lacked any part of the aforementioned trifecta. There are skills I had that applied to writing grants, encouraging a consistent work ethic with my co-workers, and organizing activities for others, like my baseball club.

My co-workers tell me I'm really talented at art, as well as the performing arts, which helps me win over the attention of the youth I work with for the theater and art clubs. Such students are marginalized from most after-school activities by their ethnicity, economic status, and even their location in the city. But the biggest part of my success is probably luck.

I am lucky in so many ways, some of which are very visible and some are just below the surface. I'm lucky that I am able to work with so many bright and personable children who inspire me to fill their heads with such ideas as civil rights, equality, and the golden rule. I'm lucky that I have colleagues who consistently break stereotypes placed upon them and are very progressive.

I am a somewhat openly* gay Volunteer, and I do not feel ostracized by the few people I have shared this information with, including some of my co-workers; it's important to mention that when working with children, you are put in a compromising situation since there are a lot of stereotypes that homosexuals are pediphiles. Thus, whether you can be open with anyone at your site or not depends. Some/most Volunteers can't be, and you definitely can't be in the beginning. I am lucky that most people I meet are supportive of me completely, whether it's a group of high school kids willing to pick up garbage with me on Thursdays or the secretary of the municipality giving me 20 boxes of clothes for the kids and families in need that we work with.

My greatest accomplishment here is that the little successes I have had were always shared with someone else as their successes, which is the way it should be, and is the real meaning of "skills transfer."

(* I need to clarify "openly gay" because, as a Peace Corps Volunteer, you receive quite a bit of attention. I do not tell Bulgarians that I am gay simply because it is a guessing game on who is going to accept it and who is going to cause you problems. I have come to Bulgaria to serve my country, to serve a population in need and to give my time to a few people who may benefit from it. I can do all of these things without addressing my sexuality to people, therefore I don't. I have a nice personal life and I do a very good job of keeping it separate from my work life.)

—*B20 Youth Development*

I remember the first, "Oh, my God, what have I done?" moment I experienced in the long process of joining the Peace Corps. I had been fine throughout the weeks and months of goodbyes—packing, visiting relatives, hosting farewell parties. I was even OK saying goodbye to my parents in the Philadelphia airport. There were a few tears, but they were quickly gone and I was looking forward to meeting the rest of my group in Chicago.

The moment the gravity of what I had signed on for hit me, we were standing in line at the Milan airport waiting to board our Sofia-bound plane. There, I heard people speaking what I could only assume was Bulgarian and started to panic. After a few minutes, I regained my composure and reminded myself that this would be a day-by-day process.

I was with a big group of people who were doing exactly the same thing I was doing, and reminded myself that I knew that we would not just be deserted by the Peace Corps.

And it was a day-by-day process. The first week of orientation seemed to last decades, and in those days I thought I could never, ever learn Bulgarian. But then we went to live with our host families, and every day I was able to communicate one more thing to my host mother. The months of training also felt like they would never end, but they did, all too soon. At the beginning, I could barely communicate to my host mom, through sign language, that I hate rice, but by the end I could tell her a (moderately) detailed history about how I had come to dislike it.

By July the whole family knew my habits, and I knew theirs. We had inside jokes and albums filled with "family" photos. But by then, it was time to become a real Peace Corps Volunteer and begin the work I had come to do.

The first months were a challenge, to say the least. My rocky Bulgarian and lack of teaching experience made going to school a very threatening idea, but I knew that if I just did it, it would get better. It did. The Bulgarians are very happy to share their culture and generosity with outsiders, so my colleagues kindly helped me learn and find my niche in the school. The students, for the most part, were unruly and disinterested, but I found a few kids who really gave me hope and kept me coming back to school every day.

I took Bulgarian lessons and went on na gosti (the Bulgarian art of visiting) and slowly came to understand the language enough to follow conversations. By the end-of-year field trip that first year, I was as much a part of the community as anyone else.

It's not easy, but no one joins the Peace Corps to do something easy. By sticking it out, I got exactly what I wanted from my Peace Corps experience—a test of my own independence, a test of my own tenacity, and an outlet to try and effect some sort of change, whether it is a student learning some English or someone realizing that not all Americans living in foreign countries wear camouflage and carry guns.

I often think about how glad I am that I did not run at that initial moment of panic. I know I would not be the same person I am today if I had not lived these past 19 months.

—*Rebecca Grudzina, B17 English Teacher (TEFL)*

PACKING LIST

This list has been compiled by Volunteers serving in Bulgaria and is based on their experience. Use it as an informal guide in making your own list, bearing in mind that experience is individual. There is no perfect list! You obviously cannot bring everything on the list, so consider those items that make the most sense to you personally and professionally. You can always have things sent to you later. As you decide what to bring, keep in mind that you have an 80-pound weight limit on baggage. And remember, you can get almost everything you need in Bulgaria.

General Clothing
Volunteers need an assortment of clothing for work, play, and socializing. Volunteers in different sites and professional roles will have different clothing requirements. Bulgarian teachers and other professionals have a fairly sophisticated fashion sense, which could be described as "elegantly casual." Your Bulgarian colleagues are the best models for what to wear in the workplace. In general, both men and women will find nice jeans dressed up with a nice shirt and jacket is acceptable in many situations.

Attire for male teachers usually consists of slacks with a nice shirt and optional tie. Female teachers will find slacks or a skirt paired with a nice shirt or sweater appropriate. COD Volunteers may find a jacket and tie *de rigueur* for the office or that slacks or a skirt, and a shirt or sweater, are more appropriate. Youth development Volunteers generally work in more casual situations, but still need appropriate business attire for special events. Suits, dresses, and skirts or nice slacks with blouses are all suitable work attire. Women should avoid clothing that requires dry cleaning because this service is not widely available. Three or four outfits shoud be sufficient for work. You will also need casual clothes for relaxing around the house, socializing, hiking, skiing, and travel. Printed or casual T-shirts and sweatshirts are fine for sports activities or for use at home, but are not usually worn for other activities.

Quality jeans (i.e. solid color and no tears) are available in Bulgaria, but they are expensive by Bulgarian standards, so you may want to bring one or two pairs of your favorite brand from the United States (dark or black jeans are preferable to light ones since they are easier to keep clean). Clothes that are comfortable and that can be layered as needed to accommodate the seasons are best. Dark clothes are easier to keep clean and hand-wash, and cotton knits are best avoided because they don't keep their shape when line-dried (plan on not having access to a clothes-dryer).

In general, most day-to-day clothing you will need can be purchased for reasonable prices in Bulgaria, so you may want to use your limited packing space to focus on specialty clothing, such as hiking apparel or sporting attire/shoes and other unique and specific items.

> ➢ Bathing suit (Bulgarian women tend to wear two-piece suits, so either two-piece or one-piece is fine)

> ➢ Two or three pairs of fleece or silk long underwear (what is available locally is not of great quality, and keep in mind that white can be difficult to clean)

- ➤ Your favorite sweater (keep in mind that good sweaters can be purchased locally at reasonable prices)

- ➤ Lightweight skirts or dresses for summer for women

- ➤ Slacks and a sports jacket or one suit and tie for men (You can alternatively purchase this here)

- ➤ A scarf, hat, and gloves (think fleece, Thinsulate, and waterproof; it gets very cold in the mountains in winter. All of these items can also be purchased locally, although it may be hard to find waterproof gloves)

- ➤ High quality warm socks, such as "smart wool" ones (you can buy socks for daily usage locally)

- ➤ Lightweight "shell" and a fleece or warm jacket that is windproof and waterproof (mid-thigh or knee-length winter coats will keep you warmer than waist-length jackets). A wool coat is easy to buy locally, but it is not easy to find a truly waterproof jacket. Jackets with removable lining may be preferable as they can be adapted for a variety of weather conditions

- ➤ Additional clothing for women who wear larger sizes. Note that it can be very challenging for female Volunteers who wear larger and tall sizes to find clothing that fits locally

- ➤ Specialty or "high-tech" sporting good clothing, including sports bra(s) for women. While day-to-day sports clothing can be purchased throughout Bulgaria, don't count on being able to easily find technical clothing such as wicking and gortex items, except for in a few pricier specialty stores in Sofia

Shoes

- ➤ For general outdoor activities, Volunteers advise that trail running-type shoes or good sneakers are adequate

- ➤ Hiking footwear: high-quality, lightweight, waterproof hiking boots are desirable if you are a serious hiker. You can buy good-quality hiking boots from major manufacturers at a few stores in Sofia

- ➤ Larger sizes: Good-quality shoes in large sizes are hard to find; women's shoes and boots are especially difficult to find in larger sizes (over size 9). If you wear a larger size, you may want to consider bringing all of the shoes you will need for your stay, including work shoes, waterproof boots, and casual shoes

- ➤ Running: If you are a runner, you'll likely want to bring good running shoes with you. While stylish athletic shoes are readily available, only a few stores in the larger cities carry high quality running shoes. Prices are expensive and sizes tend to be very limited

> Quality: The quality of much of the footwear in Bulgaria is low, although there are some high-end stores in larger cities (with high-end prices to match)

> Insoles: Dr. Scholl's type insoles can be helpful if you purchase shoes locally, as they are more often made for looks than for comfort

> Slippers (wore in Bulgarian households) and flip-flops (you'll want a pair for showering) can be easily purchased throughout Bulgaria, so no need to bring these with you

Personal Hygiene and Toiletry Items

Practically speaking, bring only enough to get through training. A wide variety of locally produced and imported items (particularly in the cities) are available in Bulgaria, so do not pack extra toothpaste, toilet paper, dental floss, and shampoo unless you are very particular about what brands you like. This goes for cosmetics, too. Some Volunteers do advise, however, that they wish they had brought more of a favorite brand of a cosmetic, lotion, or deodorant.

Kitchen

There are kitchenware stores in larger cities in Bulgaria, with practically everything you will need to equip even a gourmet kitchen; however, it might be easier and less expensive to pack some of the following:

> Favorite ethnic or local spices, such as chipotle sauce or items generally purchased at specialty or ethnic food stores

> Favorite recipes using basic ingredients (you will also receive an excellent cookbook during training that was prepared by previous Volunteers)

> Plastic measuring cups and spoons (it can be tricky using recipes with U.S. measurements and metric measuring tools)

> Rubber scrappers and spatulas (if you would be lost without them)

> Chocolate chips (although you can cut up a Bulgarian chocolate bar), marshmallows, and graham crackers are not available locally, and you can amaze your host family and Bulgarian friends with desserts (i.e. chocolate chip cookies and s'mores) made from these items

Miscellaneous

➤ Small backpack that is durable, lightweight and of good quality for overnight trips (suitcases are a nuisance and large packs may be cumbersome for short trips)

➤ Compact sleeping bag, for weekend travel and winter warmth (consider a lightweight pad too, although larger foam pads that are cheap and lightweight can be purchased locally)

➤ Laptop—Most Volunteer enjoy having laptops for personal and professional use. Remember to bring a plug adapter (to European two-prong) with a surge protector. You don't need a voltage converter, as most laptops are equipped for both 220V and 110V

➤ Camera—Most Volunteers rely on compact digital cameras, which are inconspicuous and easy to transport. To make prints you can easily bring a CD or USB device to photo shops in most towns and cities. For those who use film cameras: 35mm film (Kodak and Fuji) can be bought and developed in Bulgarian towns and cities, but not in most villages. There are very few places, even in large cities, that can process Advantix and Advanced Photo System film. Slide processing is expensive and, again, only available in the largest cities.

➤ Contact lenses and cleaning solutions (the Peace Corps does not provide contact lens supplies and they are expensive locally)

➤ Sunglasses (can be bought locally, but cheap ones can be poor quality, and expensive ones are really expensive)

➤ Sturdy, water-resistant watch with an alarm (and an extra watchband)

➤ Durable water bottle

➤ Money pouch or belt (to hide your passport and other valuables when traveling)

➤ Swiss Army knife, with a corkscrew

➤ A debit card or ATM card to withdraw cash that you know will work in Bulgaria and this region (for vacation travel)

➤ Personal checks from a U.S. checking account (handy for applications for graduate school, and for access to your checking account)

➤ Index cards (for flashcards)

- Washable markers and fun stickers if you will be teaching

- Credit card (Good for travel in other countries). Select places in Bulgaria that cater to expats now take credit cards, but there are some reports of stolen credit card numbers

- An iPod (optional, obviously, but highly recommended by many Volunteers)

- A few novels to swap and any resources related to your program that you feel you must have

- Small, durable flashlight

- Compact sewing and tool kits

- Games (Scrabble, Uno or Phase Ten, other boards games that require minimal knowledge of English, cards from a Pictionary set, Frisbee, etc.)

- Holiday and birthday cards in English to use for Bulgarian friends and colleagues

- Plastic zip-close storage bags, such as Ziploc, of various sizes (non-zip-close ones can be found in Bulgaria)

- Postcards, maps, and pictures from home to show your community and to remind you of home

- Small gifts from the U.S. or your home state for your host family and Bulgarian colleagues and friends (stickers, refrigerator magnets, postcards, key chains, pens, candy, etc.)

- Money pouch or belt (to hide your passport and other valuables when traveling)

- An American football

Note: If you bring valuable items such as a laptop, CD player, or musical instrument, bring a sales receipt or other documentation of ownership. If you or Peace Corps sends your items home as unaccompanied baggage, proof of ownership prior to your arrival in Bulgaria must be presented to Bulgarian customs officials to avoid excessive customs fees and/or export restrictions. Also remember to insure any items of value.

PRE-DEPARTURE CHECKLIST

The following list consists of suggestions for you to consider as you prepare to live outside the United States for two years. Not all items will be relevant to everyone, and the list does not include everything you should make arrangements for.

Family

- Notify family that they can call the Peace Corps' Office of Special Services at any time if there is a critical illness or death of a family member (24-hour telephone number: 800.424.8580, extension 1470).

- Give the Peace Corps' *On the Home Front* handbook to family and friends.

Passport/Travel

- Forward to the Peace Corps travel office all paperwork for the Peace Corps passport and visas.

- Verify that your luggage meets the size and weight limits for international travel.

- Obtain a personal passport if you plan to travel after your service ends. (Your Peace Corps passport will expire three months after you finish your service, so if you plan to travel longer, you will need a regular passport.)

Medical/Health

- Complete any needed dental and medical work.

- If you wear glasses, bring two pairs.

- Arrange to bring a three-month supply of all medications (including birth control pills) you are currently taking.

Insurance

- Make arrangements to maintain life insurance coverage.

- Arrange to maintain supplemental health coverage while you are away. (Even though the Peace Corps is responsible for your health care during Peace Corps service overseas, it is advisable for people who have preexisting conditions to arrange for the continuation of their supplemental health coverage. If there is a lapse in coverage, it is often difficult and expensive to be reinstated.)

- Arrange to continue Medicare coverage if applicable.

Personal Papers

- Bring a copy of your certificate of marriage or divorce.

Voting

- Register to vote in the state of your home of record. (Many state universities consider voting and payment of state taxes as evidence of residence in that state.)

- Obtain a voter registration card and take it with you overseas.

- Arrange to have an absentee ballot forwarded to you overseas.

Personal Effects

- Purchase personal property insurance to extend from the time you leave your home for service overseas until the time you complete your service and return to the United States.

Financial Management

- Keep a bank account in your name in the U.S.

- Obtain student loan deferment forms from the lender or loan service.

- Execute a Power of Attorney for the management of your property and business.

- Arrange for deductions from your readjustment allowance to pay alimony, child support, and other debts through the Office of Volunteer Financial Operations at 800.424.8580, extension 1770.

- Place all important papers—mortgages, deeds, stocks, and bonds—in a safe deposit box or with an attorney or other caretaker.

CONTACTING PEACE CORPS HEADQUARTERS

This list of numbers will help connect you with the appropriate office at Peace Corps headquarters to answer various questions. You can use the toll-free number and extension or dial directly using the local numbers provided. Be sure to leave the toll-free number and extensions with your family so they can contact you in the event of an emergency.

Peace Corps Headquarters Toll-free Number:
800.424.8580, press 2, then the extension number (see chart below)
Peace Corps Headquarters Mailing Address:
Peace Corps
Peace Corps Paul D. Coverell Peace Corps Headquarters
1111 20th St. NW
Washington, DC
20526

For Questions About:	Staff:	Toll free Extension:	Direct Number:
Responding to an Invitation	Office of Placement	Ex 1840	202.692.1840
Country and Program Information	Country Desk Officer	Ex 1184	202.696.1184
Loan Readjustments, Tax Readjustments and Power of Attorney	Office of Financial Services	Ex 1170	202.692.1170
Staging and Reporting Instructions (please note that you will receive comprehensive information, including flight and hotel information, approximately three to five weeks prior to departure)	Office of Staging	Ex 1865	202.692.1865
Family Emergencies	Office of Special Services (24-hour line)	Ex 1470	202.692.1470